the FELTED KNITS kit

INSTRUCTIONS AND TOOLS FOR 15 FANTASTIC AND FUZZY KNITTING PROJECTS

By Sara Lucas

CHRONICLE BOOKS
SAN FRANCISCO

Text © 2007 **Sara Lucas**
Photographs © 2007 **Julie Toy**
Stylist: **Jules Moore**
Illustrations © 2007 **Randy Stratton**

All rights reserved. No part of this book may be reproduced in any form without written permission from the publisher.

ISBN-10: 0-8118-5964-9
ISBN-13: 978-0-8118-5964-6

Design by **Anne Donnard**
Typeset in Barbera, Base Twelve, and Univers

Manufactured in China

Chronicle Books endeavors to use environmentally responsible paper in its gift and stationery products.

Distributed in Canada by
Raincoast Books
9050 Shaughnessy Street
Vancouver, B.C. V6P 6E5

10 9 8 7 6 5 4 3 2 1

Chronicle Books LLC
680 Second Street
San Francisco, CA 94107
www.chroniclebooks.com

PROJECTS
in this kit

01 Coasters of Many Colors
02 Calling Card Case
03 Handy Oven Mitts
04 Stained Glass Leash and Collar
05 Planter Cozy
06 Cute as a Button Napkin Rings
07 Fair Isle Glasses Case
08 "Suede" Vest
09 Golf Club Covers
10 Stash Storage Box Covers
11 Woven Ribbon Purse
12 Tweed Hat
13 Striped Duffel Bag
14 Superstar Pillow
15 Patchwork Blanket

INTRODUCTION

INTRODUCTION

I believe in covering everything with knitting, in wiggling knitting into all the spaces of life—not just the closet. And so I believe in felting. The felting process lends a whole new set of properties to knit pieces; it is like the difference between liquid and solid states. The "liquid" state, knit fabric, is pliable, stretchy, and drapey. The "solid," felted fabric, is more robust, stiff, and strong. For example, a basic knit square made in cotton is a washcloth, but when made with wool and felted, it is a potholder. Felting gives your knitting an entirely different practicality, making it appropriate for a whole new set of functions. Who can resist the magic of such transformation?

This handy kit includes projects to suit the variety of people and places in your life. You'll find the classics, such as a purse and a hat. You'll also discover some less traditional patterns: a dog collar and leash inspired by tales of felt horse bridles made long ago, a pot cozy to dress up your houseplants, and box covers to both hide and organize that oh-so-precious yarn stash. Also included are tips for pre- and post-felting fun.

Felting can really show off knitting techniques such as Fair Isle and lace sequences. And the embellishment options are virtually limitless. The projects here feature less extravagant detailing, but feel free to ham it up to your heart's content.

Knitting is all about expression, a way of putting yourself in the world. You choose the colors, the attitude, the textures. And felting is one more way to achieve your vision.

GLOSSARY
of abbreviations

GLOSSARY OF ABBREVIATIONS

*	repeat as many times as is indicated or until end of row
beg	beginning
BO	bind off
CC	contrast color
CO	cast on
inc	increase
K	knit
Kf&b	knit into the front then back of next stitch (see Special Techniques, page 20)
K2tog	knit two together (see Special Techniques, page 20)
knitwise	as if to knit
M1	make one. M1R is right-slanting, M1L is left-slanting, M1P is made as if to purl (see Special Techniques, page 22).
MC	main color
P	purl
PM	place marker
psso	pass the slipped stitch over (as in binding off)
p2sso	pass the 2 slipped stitches over (just like psso but with 2 stitches)
PU&K	pick up and knit (see Special Techniques, page 24)
rem	remaining
Rep(s)	repeat(s)
Rnd(s)	round(s)
RS	right side, public side

SSK	slip one stitch knitwise, slip second stitch knitwise, knit slipped stitches together tbl (see Special Techniques, page 27)
St st	stocking or stockinette stitch (knit on RS, purl on WS)
tbl	through the back loop
W&T	wrap and turn (See Special Techniques, Short Rows, page 25.)
WS	wrong side, inside
wyif/b	with yarn in front/back
yo	yarn over

TECHNIQUES

The following are brief overviews of the techniques used in this kit. Please see the Resources section for sources of information on any techniques that you can't figure out from my instructions. Of course, a good way to learn a new technique is to ask a fellow knitter, or stop by your local yarn store for a quick tutorial. I've divided these techniques into three sections: Felting, Basic, and Special, which are listed on the following pages.

FELTING TECHNIQUES

The basic equation of felting is simple: **WOOL + HOT WATER + FRICTION = FELT.** The hot water helps open the scales on the fiber, and the friction causes the scales to tangle and lock onto each other. Most of the time, the washing machine provides the water and friction, you provide the wool, and *voilà!*—felt emerges. In some regards, the process really is that straightforward . . . and in some ways it isn't. Felting is more finicky than the basic equation above indicates. A change in yarn, water temperature, or even color can affect felting. (Which is not to say that you shouldn't try your own color combos for the projects in this kit—I encourage color play whenever possible!) Here are some tips for successful felting.

The first thing to think about is the **yarn** you want to use. It should be mostly animal fiber and mostly untreated. **Wool**, **mohair**, **alpaca**, **cashmere**, and **angora** all felt well as long as they haven't been bleached or made into super-wash. I say mostly animal fiber because a certain amount of nylon, for example, will not impede the felting process and can actually add some interesting texture. Many felted purse patterns use nylon carry-alongs as trim. **Silk** felts to a certain degree, but silk yarn will definitely change the "feltedness" of the finished fabric. This has been exploited in the blanket pattern in this kit—a yarn with quite a bit of silk is recommended to keep the blanket from felting entirely and becoming too stiff.

Next you will need to choose a **needle**. You should generally use a needle **at least two sizes bigger** than the ball band on the yarn calls for. If you knit a piece too tightly, the fiber won't have room to open and move around. In other words, you will have inhibited the friction part of the equation. That said, you might have a stitch pattern that you don't want to felt into oblivion. As long as the stitch pattern is more important than how firm your felt is, you can knit the piece with the normal needle size or one size up.

Which brings up a very important point. Few steps are more important and more often skimped on than **swatching**. I have one thing to say about this: Do big swatches! You may find you tend to knit differently on a little swatch than on the longer rows of a project. So to get an accurate swatch, it needs to be bigger. This is even truer when it comes to felting because a bigger piece of fabric will felt differently (usually more) than a smaller piece. There are two solutions: First, make what will be a generous swatch even after it has been felted. You may want to buy an extra ball of yarn so you have plenty to play with. Remember, you can't just tear out your piece and re-knit it if it comes out of the washing machine the wrong size. And really, is an extra ball of yarn too much to pay for peace of mind? Second, do not rely solely on your swatch for sizing, although it will give you an idea if you will need half a wash cycle or two and a half cycles. You must keep a close eye on your piece as it felts so you can yank it out of the washing machine as soon as it is the right size.

Now, the easy part—the **knitting**. Because it is going to shrink, you will often make your piece three times as big as the desired size. And because stitch patterns don't show much after felting, you will usually knit in stockinette stitch. That means rows and rows (or rounds and rounds) of "relaxation knitting." Felting also allows you to skimp a little on some of the details. Although I recommend fully fashioned decreases whenever appropriate, if you get one wrong, it won't show. You can also use bar increases instead of make-one (M1) increases and you won't have to worry if an increase messes up your seed stitch a little. Like I said, it's effortless knitting.

Once you have knit your giant and you are ready to knock it down to size, into the **washing machine** it goes. Of course, the whole process is easier to control with a top-load machine, but most home-version front loaders will let you stop midcycle and open the door. If your local laundry has only front loaders, pick a neighborhood you have always wanted to visit and use the Laundromat there. Felting may take a little longer in a Laundromat because the water is seldom as hot as it is at home.

Set the washing machine control to hot wash, cold rinse. You may or may not use much of the rinse cycle, but cold is good for setting the fibers. Most felting experts will advise you to set the water level to high. However, I suggest medium, because I think it works just as well and wastes less water. Add a pair of jeans for increased agitation. Launder with a little dish or laundry liquid, or a wool wash. The advantage to wool wash is that you don't have to rinse it out—as soon as your piece is felted to the desired size, you are finished. You can add a little vinegar (or even soak your piece in vinegar before washing) to help set the colors. Check your piece every five minutes (less as it gets closer to size). Conventional wisdom recommends avoiding the spin cycle as it can cause creases, but I have to admit I put everything through the spin cycle. I have never had problems with creases, but I believe others when they say they have. If you don't want to chance it, squeeze out excess water with a towel and lay the piece out to dry.

Once you take your piece out of the washing machine, stretch and shape it according to the size and shape you want. This is an incredibly important step and can make or break your results. Take your time and check measurements, too. While your piece is still wet, you can really affect the size and shape. For example, the coasters were squared up, and the star pillow rounds were coaxed into a rounder shape.

If you need to put some finishing touches on a piece, or if one part isn't felting properly in the washing machine, hand felting is a good way to go. That way you have more control over which sections felt and how much. You just need some gloves, hot water, soap, and time. Fill a sink or a bucket or a roasting pan with hot water and a little soap and get comfortable. You will probably have to swish and squeeze and pat the area to be felted for quite some time before you see results.

In felting, as in knitting, there is definitely an aspect of trial and error, and some possibility of the happy, or even unhappy, accident. After all, that is part of the magic!

BASIC TECHNIQUES AND TERMS

Slipknot: This is a very useful item in knitting and elsewhere in life. It is how you start a crochet chain and many of the cast-on methods in knitting.

To make a slipknot, pretend you are going to tie a half knot, but don't pull the free end all the way through. Instead a loop forms and you tighten it by pulling on the working yarn. In other words, hold the yarn in your left hand where you want the knot. With your right hand, drape the tail over the working yarn. Reach through the loop and pull the tail through, stopping before the end comes through (see figure 1a). Tighten by pulling on the working yarn. Fit the loop over the needle or hook and tighten gently by pulling on the tail end (see figure 1b).

Cast On: See Cable Cast On, Half Hitch Cast On, Knitted Cast On, and Long-tail Cast On in the Special Techniques section.

Bind Off (Cast Off): This is how you end most knitted pieces. As with other techniques in knitting, there are a bunch of different ways to bind off. This is the most common, and will serve you well for most projects.

Work two stitches, one at a time, in pattern. With the left-hand needle, pick up the first stitch you worked (the one closest to your right hand) and bring it over the second stitch and off the tip of both needles. Work one more stitch so that there are two stitches on the right-hand needle. Repeat the leapfrog of first stitch over second stitch and off. When you have only one stitch left on the right-hand needle, cut your yarn and pull it through the stitch.

figure 1a

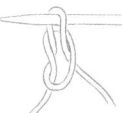

figure 1b

Knit: There are two basic stitches in knitting, and "knit" is usually considered the first or primary stitch. It is a little easier for most people, and is used more when knitting in the round. The knit stitch looks like a V.

The yarn can be held in either the right hand or the left hand. It is called Continental style if you hold the yarn in the left hand, and English style if you hold the yarn in the right hand. Both styles have their advantages and disadvantages. Continental is often faster, especially on ribbing and other similar stitch patterns. English is easier to learn and is easier for decreases, pick up and knit, and other stitch manipulations.

To make a knit stitch, hold the full needle in the left hand and the empty needle in the right hand. Insert the tip of the empty needle into the first stitch from left to right, from front to back. Wrap the working yarn around the back needle (the right-hand needle) counterclockwise. Draw the loop through the stitch to the front of the work. This is the new stitch. Now slide the old stitch from the left-hand needle.

Purl: A purl stitch is the reverse, or back side, of a knit stitch. When you make a knit stitch on one side, it appears as a purl stitch on the other. A purl stitch looks like a horizontal bar or bump.

To make a purl stitch, insert the needle from right to left, in front of the work with the yarn in front. Wrap the yarn around the right-hand needle in front of the work counterclockwise, the same way as you did for knit. Draw the loop through the stitch. Then slide the old stitch off the left needle.

Gauge: Gauge, or tension, is a way of describing how thick a yarn is, and/or how tightly it is knit. It is expressed in terms of stitches and rows per inch. A thicker yarn will have fewer stitches per inch than a thinner yarn, because each stitch is bigger. Similarly, a thin yarn knit on big needles will have fewer stitches per inch than that same yarn knit on small needles.

To measure gauge, lay a tape measure or ruler on the fabric somewhere that is most representative of the overall fabric. If you measure too close to any edge or a change in stitch pattern, you will get incorrect results. It is a good idea to count the number of stitches over at least two inches and then divide the count accordingly to get the number of stitches per inch. In fact, most patterns and ball bands will give the number of stitches and rows over a 4-inch (10 cm) square. If you are substituting yarns, compare the specified gauge to that given on the ball band.

Gauge in the Round: Because some people knit with different tension than they purl, it can be important to do a round swatch for a round project. Elizabeth Zimmermann took swatching in the round to the extreme: For a sweater in the round, her swatch would be a baby hat. You can do a swatch in the round even if you don't want to go quite that far. On circular or double-pointed needles, cast on a generous number of stitches—at least 6 more than you would for a flat swatch. This is because the edges will be very loose and you don't want to have to measure anywhere near them. Knit across the row, then slide the stitches back to the other point so that the right side is still facing you and the working yarn is at the opposite end. Pulling the working yarn loosely across the back of the work, knit across the row again in the same direction.

READING YOUR WORK

It is important to be able to read your work, which means being able to tell where you are in a stitch pattern by looking at the stitches. This will save you a lot of counting and anxiety. You will also be able to see, and therefore fix, mistakes more quickly and easily. On the most basic level, you need to be able to distinguish a knit stitch from a purl. A knit stitch looks like a V, and a purl looks like a horizontal bar or bump. It is also very helpful to be able to recognize where you have decreased or increased. Recognizing yarnovers, slipped stitches, or how many stitches you have bound off is all part of reading your work. This skill, like any other, comes with practice. For example, next time you decrease, work a couple stitches past the decrease and then look back to see what it looks like. Look again after a row or two and see what it looks like then, etc.

Of course we will all take as much help as we can get. Row counters (or tally marks with pencil and paper) are a great help for keeping track of rows. And stitch markers can separate sections within a row, like a border from the main body of a piece, or one repeat from another.

SPECIAL TECHNIQUES

Blocking: This is one of those mythical things that everyone has heard of, but many know nothing about. The process is simple: Pin (don't use pins that will rust!) the knitted piece to the specified dimensions, spray, and let dry. Alternatively, instead of spraying it wet, you can hover over it with your steam iron (don't ever let the iron touch the knitting). The effect is to set your stitches, to correct small shaping problems, or to stretch (within reason) a knitted piece to desired measurements. Sometimes blocking is like magic, somehow transforming your knitting into gold. Sometimes, however, it is just more trouble than it is worth. For example, wool and animal fibers block better than cotton, which blocks better than man-made materials. If you have a novelty yarn scarf, don't bother to block. If, on the other hand, you have the pieces for an Aran sweater in wool, take the time to block it well. You will be amply rewarded.

Cable Cast On: Cable cast on is very similar to knitted cast on. It forms a tighter, but more elastic, edge. Cable cast on leaves you ready to start a knit row, which can be handy for following charts. Like the knitted cast on, cable cast on doesn't need a long tail. To begin this cast-on method, you need two stitches made using any cast on you want. Cable cast on is done just like the knitted cast on, but instead of inserting the needle into the stitch, you insert it between the two stitches. Wrap the yarn around the needle and draw the loop between the stitches to the front. Place this new stitch onto the left needle. Insert the right-hand needle between the two stitches closest to the tip before you tighten the loop/stitch you just made. It is easier to insert the needle this way, and it will help to keep an even tension for your cast on. If you place the new stitch on the needle from the top (as if purling from left to right) you will get a looser edge. If you place it on from the bottom (as if knitting from left to right) you will get a slightly tighter edge.

Fair Isle (or Jacquard): This is the knitting technique that consists of using two colors in the same row to make a pattern. The color not in use is carried (sometimes called "floated" or "stranded") across the back of the work, so it is not practical to use this method for large, uninterrupted sections of color. For these, a technique called intarsia is used.

The most efficient way to do Fair Isle is to knit the background color using the Continental method of knitting and the contrast color using the English method; this means that you work with one color held in each hand. It is worth learning to do this because it will improve your speed. Fair Isle can also be done with two colors in one hand, either with or without a yarn guide (a knitting gadget worn on your finger to separate and tension the two colors). Whichever way you do it, be sure not to pull the floats too tightly as this will pucker the fabric. As you knit, you should spread the finished stitches along your right needle to ensure that the floats are long enough for the work to lay flat.

Fully Fashioned Decreases: This is a concept that helps your garment look more symmetrical and professional. We know that decreases slant, and this is how we put those slants to work. It goes like this: Any time you decrease, you will do it one (or two or however many stitches you want as long as it is consistent throughout the garment) stitch from the edge, and you will do it symmetrically. This means using K2tog at one side of the row and SSK at the other. Usually, the decrease is set to slant away from the edge you are creating. So SSK, slanting left, is used at the beginning of a RS armhole row, and K2tog, slanting right, is used at the end of the row. Similarly, K2tog is used at the neck edge of the left side and SSK is used at the neck edge of the right side. This way the decreases become part of the overall aesthetic of the garment, instead of something you want to hide. Also, it makes it easier to sew seams or pick up necklines if the decreases are not right on the edge.

Half Hitch (or Backward Loop) Cast On: This is the easiest cast on to do, but the first row of knitting after casting on this way is a pain. Half hitch cast on is very useful, however, for casting on a few stitches in the middle of a row, as in buttonholes, gloves and mittens, and certain gussets.

To cast on this way, start with a slipknot on the needle, or if you are in the middle of a row, just work the cast on next. Hold onto the working yarn in your left hand and the needle in your right. Extend the left index finger parallel to the yarn, then dip your finger under the yarn and toward you. Move the tip of the needle from the base of your finger toward the finger tip so that the needle is through the loop with your finger. Remove your finger and tighten the loop around the needle.

I-cord: Lke the name suggests, I-cord is a cord or tube like a thick, knitted string. It is useful as a tie or drawstring, a handle for a bag, or even as a ribbon for a present. It can also be sewn or applied to an edge for a nice finished look, or coiled to make anything from a frog closure to a potholder.

You can make I-cord with a circular needle, but it is much faster with two double-pointed needles. Cast on the desired number of stitches (usually 3 or 4) and knit across them. Now, instead of turning your work as you normally would, slide the stitches to the opposite end of the needle with the same side still facing you. The working yarn will be at the "wrong" end of the needle. Knit the stitches in the same order again, pulling the working yarn around behind the stitches fairly tightly when knitting the first stitch. This will draw the knitting into a cord or tube.

Intarsia: Intarsia is colorwork that consists of knitting isolated areas of color. For example, if you wanted to make a diamond in the middle of a sweater, you would use intarsia. For each area of color, you need a separate ball of yarn. If you are doing a fairly simple or large pattern, you can just keep using yarn from the original balls (as long as you have as many balls as you have sections of color). If you were doing something with multiple small blocks of color, like allover polka dots, you would want to wind a portion of yarn off the ball and onto a bobbin, then use a separate bobbin for each color section. Because you knit each section with its own yarn supply, intarsia is worked generally flat (back and forth), not in the round.

To work intarsia, knit across to the place the colors are going to change. Drop the old color and pick up the new. To lock the two colors together and avoid leaving a hole at the color change, the yarns must be twisted around each other. Bring the new color under the old color to catch the old color. There are other tips about twisting the two yarns, and just about every book will recommend something different. If you use common sense, and examine your knitting as you go to be sure it looks good, the results will be OK.

Both Fair Isle and intarsia colorwork techniques are usually expressed in the form of a chart, one square representing each stitch. If you are having trouble keeping your place on the chart, you can photocopy it and mark it up as you go. One way to do this is to divide the chart into sections, and place markers in the knitting to correspond to your chart divisions. This way, you only have to keep track of a limited number of stitches at a time.

The "Jogless" Jog: I learned this from Meg Swansen's column in one of the first knitting magazines I ever bought, so I always get a little thrill of discovery using it. When knitting in the round, you are actually working in a very shallow spiral. Thus, when you change colors, the first stitch and the last stitch of the round don't line up exactly. This little un-invention corrects that. On the first stitch of the second round of the new color, pick up the old-colored stitch below the new-colored stitch that is on the needle and knit the two together. This lengthens the old-color stitch enough to bring it up level with the end of the last old-colored row.

Joining in the Round: Joining in the round is like a snake eating its tail. The first stitch that was cast on is also the first stitch you knit. After casting on, spread the stitches evenly around the needle. The side with the working yarn attached to it should be in the right hand (just as if you were in the middle of a row). Check to be sure that the stitches are not twisted in a spiral around the needles. In other words, the tops of the stitches should all be on top of the needle. Place a marker on the right-hand needle and knit into the first stitch on the left-hand needle. When you come around to the marker the next time, slip it to the right-hand needle. Check once more that the stitches are not twisted and proceed. Hereafter, you don't have to worry about the stitches getting twisted. Remember, when you are working in the round, you never see the wrong side of the fabric. So, to make stockinette stitch, you just have to knit (no purling!). To make garter stitch, you have to knit one round, purl one round.

Knit into the Front and Back (inc or Kf&b): This increase, also known as the bar increase, is fairly quick to do but leaves a purl bump on the knit side of the fabric. For this reason it is best used on garter or reverse stockinette stitch, with fuzzy or bumpy yarn, or in places where it either will not bother you or will make a decorative pattern.

To work this increase, insert the needle into the next stitch and wrap the yarn as if making a regular knit stitch. Draw the wrap through the stitch like a regular knit stitch, but do not slip the old stitch off the left needle. Now swivel the right needle so that it is behind the left needle and insert it into the back loop of the same stitch. Wrap the yarn, draw the wrap through the stitch, and slip the old stitch off the left needle.

Knit (Purl) Two Together (K2tog/P2tog): This one is easy. Just insert the right-hand needle into the next two stitches instead of just into the next one. Complete the stitch as normal. This is a right-slanting decrease but is commonly used when slant is not a factor.

Knitted Cast On: This cast on makes a somewhat loose edge, which makes it perfect for stitches that you want to pick up later. It is very easy to perform: If you can knit, you can do this cast on.

Start with a slipknot on the left needle. This cast on only uses one tail of yarn, so the slipknot can be close to the end. Insert the right needle into the slipknot as if to knit. Wrap as you would normally when knitting and draw the loop through to the front. Instead of slipping the old stitch off the left needle, put the new stitch on the left needle next to it to form a new stitch. To cast on the next stitch, insert the right needle into the stitch you just made, wrap as if to knit, draw the loop through, and place the new loop on the left needle again. If you are casting on in the middle of a piece, simply omit the slipknot and begin the cast on by knitting into the first stitch on the left needle.

Long-Tail or Two-Tail Cast On: Long-tail cast on is very versatile and is the cast on most people use most of the time. In its usual form, it makes a cast-on edge and a row of knit at the same time, although there is a way to do it so that it forms a row of purl. One drawback to this cast on is that it uses two ends of yarn, so you have to estimate how long the tail should be based on how many stitches you need. The more stitches you will cast on, the longer the tail should be. It has been said that you should make the tail three to four times as long as the width of the cast-on edge. If you are not afraid of running out of yarn for the project, give the tail a little extra. It is very frustrating to run out of tail three or four stitches shy of the end and have to start all over again. For a very wide project, like a blanket, you can do this cast on with two balls of yarn, then continue knitting with just one of them; that way you don't have to try to guess how much you'll use.

To start the long-tail cast on, pull out the desired tail length and make a slipknot. Place this slipknot on one needle, and hold that needle in your right hand. This counts as the first stitch. With the left hand, make a fist around the two tails, then split these open with your thumb and forefinger to form a triangle (needle, thumb, forefinger; see figure 2a, page 22). Holding onto the stitch on the needle with your right thumb or fore-finger, move the needle down toward your palm, with the point facing up. This forms sort of a slingshot shape (see figure 2b, page 22). Move the tip of the needle from the base of your thumb up toward the tip so that it goes through the loop on your thumb, go counterclockwise around the yarn that is on the index finger, and then back down your thumb from tip to base (see figure 2c). This last part will feel a bit like you are undoing it. Now remove your thumb from the loop and tighten it to the needle. As with most cast ons, do not make it too tight because the cast-on edge has less elasticity than the knitted fabric. If you make it too tight, the fabric will spread out above the cast on in a very unattractive way.

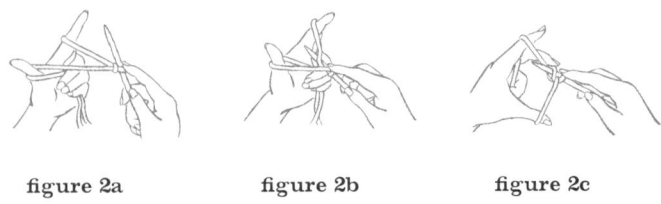

figure 2a   figure 2b   figure 2c

Make One (M1): This increase is relatively smooth and solid, which makes it a good choice for a variety of situations. Since it does slant subtly, it can be used in pairs for symmetry. Since the slant is subtle, you can use the M1R alone for situations in which the increases don't line up, are not too close together and not right above each other.

M1R—To make the right-slanting version, insert the left needle from back to front under the horizontal strand between the stitch on the left needle and the stitch on the right needle. To avoid making a hole, knit or purl this through the front (as you normally would) to twist the stitch as you knit (or purl) it.

M1L—Insert the left needle from front to back under the strand between the two stitches. In this case, in order to twist the stitch, you must knit or purl it through the back loop.

M1P—Make one purlwise is basically the same idea. Insert the needle from back to front under the strand between the stitches and purl into the front of the stitch like normal.

Mattress Stitch or Invisible Seam: There are many ways to sew pieces together, but mostly we use mattress stitch. It basically creates a row or column of knitting in between the two pieces. When done well on a vertical-to-vertical seam, it cannot be seen from the right side.

Vertical to Vertical (like side seams)—Insert the yarn needle in between the first and second stitches on the edge. Pick up two "ladder rungs" and pull the yarn through. Go to the other piece and pick up the corresponding rungs on that side. Continue going back and forth from piece to piece, being sure to insert the needle into the fabric at the same place you came out on the last pass. (See figure 3a.)

Horizontal to Horizontal—Insert the needle just inside the cast-on or bound-off edge and pick up the two strands that make the V of a knit stitch (near the bottom of the point of the V where the strands meet, not at the top of the V). Insert under the corresponding stitch on the other piece. Work back and forth in this manner, always inserting the needle back into the fabric where it came out the time before. (See figures 3b and 3c.)

Horizontal to Vertical—On one piece you will insert into the fabric and pick up the ladder rungs (as for Vertical to Vertical), and on the other side you will pick up the V of a stitch (as for Horizontal to Horizontal). Because the ratio of rows to stitches is not equal, you will not always take two rungs for every V. Usually, it is something like one V,

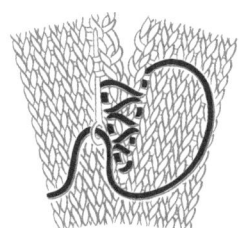

figure 3a

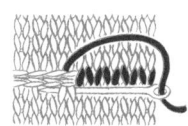

figure 3b

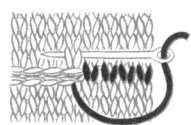

figure 3c

two rungs, one V, one rung. Experiment to see what gives the most even results, and always insert the needle into the fabric where it came out before, even if you are trying to make up ground on one or the other piece. (See figure 3d.)

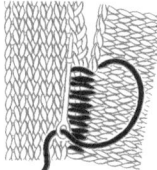

figure 3d

Needle Felting: Needle felting is one of the easiest methods of embellishment—it takes very little skill to get the basics and is really forgiving. If ever you don't like something, just pull it off or reshape it.

The needles are very sharp and have small triangles cut into them, sort of reverse barbs. As you pass the needle in and out of the wool, the fibers are enmeshed. That is all there is to it. At least, that's all there is to getting started, and it's all you need for the basic embellishments. Once you feel ready to experiment, sculpt, or soak in some extra inspiration there are plenty of books you can turn to. Just be sure you always have a piece of foam to protect your hand or leg. And never look away from the needle while using it. Unlike knitting needles, these puppies are sharp.

Pick Up and Knit (PU&K): This is how you bring dead edges to life. You'll see it at necklines, sock gussets, and armholes. Perform PU&K with the right side of the fabric facing you. With one needle in the right hand, insert the needle tip through the fabric, at least two strands from the edge. Wrap (with the same motion you use to knit) the working yarn around the needle and draw this loop through the fabric to the front/right side.

If you find this difficult, you can also use a crochet hook to help. Stick the crochet hook into the fabric from the right side, as described above, grab the working yarn with it, pull it back to the right side, then slip it to your knitting needle.

Most patterns will tell you how many stitches to pick up, and you just need to be sure you pick them up evenly. Of course, there is some leeway. If there is a spot that is a little loose or would create a hole if you used it to pick up, skip that space and use the next one.

If your pattern doesn't tell you how many stitches to pick up, do not despair. If you are picking up along a cast-on or bound-off edge it is easy—just pick up one stitch for every stitch along the edge. If you are picking up along a vertical edge, some quick math is all you need. Simply compare the stitch gauge to the row gauge. For example, if you have 5 stitches and 7 rows per inch, you want to pick up 5 stitches for every 7 rows along the edge. You could pick up 2, skip one, pick up 3, skip one. You could also measure your edge and mark every inch or two. According to our example here of 5 stitches per inch, in every 2-inch space you would need to pick up 10 stitches.

Purl Two Together Through the Back Loops (P2tog tbl): This requires a bit of contortion, but is the most popular left-leaning purl decrease. With the right-hand needle, reach around the back and all the way to the left of the next two stitches. Insert the needle from the back into the first two stitches from left to right so the point emerges in the front. Wrap the yarn as if to purl, and complete the stitch.

Short Rows: A short row is a row that does not get worked all the way to the end. Instead, you work back and forth in the middle of the row. This shaping technique has the effect of putting extra fabric in the center of a piece. This can be useful for everything from bust darts to heels and shoulder shaping.

To work a short row, work across the row as directed, then turn work around and work in the opposite direction. To avoid leaving a gap at the spot where you turn, you "wrap" a stitch. Depending on what book you read you will get differing opinions on how to wrap a stitch. One way is as follows: Knit specified number of stitches, slip the next stitch purlwise, move yarn to front of work, slip stitch back to left needle, move yarn to back of work, turn work. A second way is as follows: Knit specified number of stitches, move yarn to front of work, slip the next stitch purlwise, move yarn to back of work, slip stitch back to left needle. I prefer the former method.

The second part of short row shaping is to pick up the wraps. In other words, after you have worked the desired number of short rows, you usually will go back to knitting full rows. As you do the first full row, you will want to pick up the wraps so they do not show. To pick up a wrap on the knit side, knit to the wrapped stitch, insert the right needle into the wrap from underneath (knitwise), then insert into the stitch on the needle and knit these two together. To pick up a wrap on the purl side, insert the right needle into the back loop of the wrap (that is, from underneath and behind), place the wrap on the left-hand needle, then purl these two together.

Some short rows, like those on a traditional heel, work together with decreases to achieve a decorative diagonal effect. These short rows avoid holes by decreasing across the gap that is formed by turning the work.

Slip 1 (sl 1): This is one of the easiest instructions and for that very reason, it can be confusing. To slip a stitch is just to move it from one needle to the other, usually from the left to the right. You can slip a stitch knitwise or purlwise—putting your needle in as if to knit before you slip makes it knitwise, putting your needle in as if to purl makes it purlwise. Always slip a stitch purlwise unless slipping knitwise is specified—this keeps it untwisted and ready for the next row.

Slip, Slip, Knit (SSK): SSK is a left-slanting decrease. There are two ways to do SSK (at least). Traditionally it goes like this: Slip two stitches knitwise one at a time, insert the left needle into the front of these two slipped stitches (like a purl going backward), wrap the yarn around the back/right-hand needle and complete the knit stitch. The second way is to slip the first stitch knitwise and the second purlwise.

Surface Crochet: This is a great way to add decoration to the surface of your knitting. I think it is also the easiest way to write on your knitting. Set yourself up with the right side of the fabric facing you, the yarn underneath the fabric on the wrong side, and your crochet hook in front on the right side. Insert the hook through the fabric and pull a loop of yarn through to the front. Move forward along the fabric a little, insert the hook through, grab another loop of yarn, and pull it through to the front and through the loop on the hook. The movement is very much like performing a crochet slip stitch. It may take a little experimentation to get the tension and distances right, and this will depend on the size of the yarn, the hook size, and the look you want.

Three-Needle Bind Off: Three-needle bind off is a combination seam and bind off. It can be useful in many places, most usually as an alternative to binding off and seaming at the shoulders of a sweater. With three-needle bind off, you work a stitch from the front piece together with a stitch from the back, so you can be sure everything will line up. Another advantage is that it is one less seam to sew later. On the other hand, a three-needle bind off is not quite as stable as a traditional seam, so if you have very heavy sleeves, three-needle bind off may not be the best seam.

To perform three-needle bind off you need, as the name suggests, three needles (or two needles and a crochet hook of the same size). Arrange the two pieces with their right sides together and with the needle points facing the same direction (toward the right, if you are knitting right-handed). With the third needle or the crochet hook knit or purl (as the stitch dictates) a stitch from the front needle together with a stitch from the back needle. Repeat this once more so there are two stitches on the right-hand needle, and then bind off the first stitch on the right needle as you normally would. Continue in this way until one stitch remains on the right needle. Cut the yarn and pull the tail through the last stitch to fasten it off.

Two Circular Needles: Not too long ago, the sock-knitting world was revolutionized by Cat Bordi and her book *Socks Soar on Two Circular Needles.* She had "unvented" a way to make socks without double-pointed needles. I don't make socks exactly like she does, but I am a strong advocate for the two-circular-needles approach to knitting just about anything that used to involve double-points.

The two circulars do not have to be the same length. In fact, if they are different, it is easier to tell them apart, and it is more economical not to invest in two of the exact same needle. You can also mark or color your needles so you know which two ends belong to which needle if you find yourself perplexed each time you need to switch needles.

Arrange the stitches so that about half are on each circular needle. Knit across the stitches on the first needle, using both ends of the same needle. After completing the stitches on the first needle, slide them onto the plastic cord. This needle will now act as a stitch holder as you work across the stitches on the second needle. Move the stitches on the second needle from the cord to the needle tip so they are ready to knit.

Knit across this half of the stitches, using the two needle points of the same circular. The yarn will come from the back needle to the front needle to make the first stitch. This is what keeps the two sides connected and forms the knitted tube. Make sure that you work the first stitch firmly to prevent a ladder from forming. Continue like this, alternating needles, as you work your sock.

It is easier to get the hang of this technique if you don't have to worry about the cast-on edge twisting, so try it first on a piece that is already started in the round, like the top of a hat.

Whipstitch: Whipstitch is certainly not the cleanest or smoothest seaming method but can make a very cute decorative edge, especially when a contrasting color or textured yarn is used. It is also very easy.

Holding the two pieces with their wrong sides together, insert the needle through both fabrics, front to back. Bring the needle back around to the front, wrapping the yarn over the top of the edges. Repeat. Be sure to insert into the same column or row of stitches for the whole seam.

Whipstitch can also be used to appliqué or to overlap two pieces. Insert the needle through the background near the edge of the appliqué or top piece. Come up through the background and appliqué, near the edge. Usually you see this done at a slight angle, but it can be done with straight stitches as well.

Yarn Over (yo): A yarn over is a way of increasing. It is definitely the easiest increase, but it leaves a hole so it is only appropriate in some cases. To perform a yarn over, you just do what it says: Wrap the yarn over the right-hand needle to create a new loop on the needle. On the following row, work the yarn over like an ordinary stitch. It is like making a knit stitch without inserting into the next stitch.

RESOURCES

RESOURCES

There are so many great knitting books it is hard to know where to start and even harder to know when to stop. Below are a few that got on the list for being great overall references, excellent on specific themes, timeless classics, or particularly useful to have around. If you can't afford to amass a personal knitting library, your local public library will be a great resource.

Magazines are also great sources of information and inspiration. Not only are they often full of mouthwatering projects, but most magazines will have at least one technique discussion per issue. Your local bookstore will probably have a couple of the more mainstream magazines, and your local yarn store will probably have a ton of choices. I love *Interweave Knits* and *Vogue Knitting*, to name a couple. There are also brand-affiliated magazines, like *Rowan* and *Rebecca*, which come out twice a year.

And don't overlook the online magazines, blogs, and other great sites. Knitters love community, and the Internet is as community-fostering as it gets. A couple faves are "Knitty" and "ABCs of Knitting." If you need additional help, don't understand something I have written, or just want to chat, feel free to e-mail me at felting@yarnofthemonth.com. I am always happy to talk about knitting.

BOOKS

Felted Knits by Beverly Galeskas (Interweave Press, 2003)

Feltmaking Projects for Children by Anne Einset Vickery (Craft Works, 2003)

Knitted Embellishments by Nicky Epstein (Interweave Press, 1999)

Knitter's Almanac by Elizabeth Zimmermann (Schoolhouse Press, 1974)

The Knitter's Companion by Vicki Square (Interweave Press, 1996)

The Knitter's Handy Book of Patterns by Ann Budd (Interweave Press, 2002)

Knitting Around by Elizabeth Zimmermann (Schoolhouse Press, 1981)

Knitting from the Top by Barbara Walker (Schoolhouse Press, 1972)

Knitting Without Tears by Elizabeth Zimmermann (Schoolhouse Press, 1971)

Needle Felting Art Techniques and Projects by Anne Einset Vickery with Patricia Spark and Linda Van Alstyne (Craft Works Publishing, 2002)

Simply Felt: 20 Easy and Elegant Designs in Wool by Margaret Docherty and Jayne Emerson (Interweave Press, 2004)

Socks Soar on Two Circular Needles by Cat Bordi (Passing Paws Press, 2001)

Stitch & Bitch by Debbie Stoller (Workman, 2003)

Treasury of Knitting Patterns (1981), **A Second Treasury of Knitting Patterns** (1998), **Charted Knitting Designs** (1998), **Fourth Treasury of Knitting Patterns** (2000) by Barbara Walker (Schoolhouse Press)

Vogue Knitting Ultimate Knitting Book (Pantheon Books, 2002)